Writing ~~This~~ Won't Hurt a Bit!

Painless remedies for English ailments

LINDSAY C LEWIS

 FriesenPress

Suite 300 - 990 Fort St
Victoria, BC, Canada, V8V 3K2
www.friesenpress.com

ISBN
978-1-4602-7220-6 (Hardcover)
978-1-4602-7221-3 (Paperback)
978-1-4602-7222-0 (eBook)

1. Juvenile Nonfiction, Language Arts,
Composition & Creative Writing

Distributed to the trade by The Ingram Book Company

Table of Contents

Foreword

I first met Lindsay Lewis in 1994 when she co-founded an ESL Summer Institute at St. Michaels University School. After a number of years of teaching at colleges and universities, she returned to private English tutoring at the corporate and high school level. She is always closely engaged with her students' lives and targets their learning so that they gain confidence and improve quickly.

There are many 'help books' on English Grammar and Usage but they can be dry, intimidating and perhaps too formal in their approach to maintain students' interest. Teachers write comments such as 'vague' 'elaborate' and 'not clear' which are of little help. This book takes those types of comments and gives concrete examples of how writing can be improved. Lindsay brings to this book the same passion as she does to her classes using clever humour and amusing, simple examples as the key elements in the explanations.

'This Won't Hurt a Bit' really does provide painless remedies for English ailments and is a must read. By providing simple, concrete examples to which the reader can relate, students of English will not only learn but also enjoy the process. After using this book you will understand not only your ailments but also their remedies.

Peter G. Gardiner BSc. M.A.

Associate Director of Advancement

St. Michaels University School

Winner of the Prime Minister's Award for Teaching Excellence

Food for Thought

Imagine eating a thick, juicy, grilled hamburger, hot off the BBQ. The meaty aroma fills the air as you slather the charred beef with ketchup, mustard, lettuce, sliced tomato and sizzling bacon.

Vegans may prefer a smoked tofu wrap with grated carrot, cucumber and tomato topped with Thai peanut sauce.

Are you hungry? Can you taste the mouth-watering burger? Why? You are merely reading words on a page.

I have just demonstrated the power of language.

Words are the meat and potatoes of communication and grammar is the sauce, ranging from the humble gravy to a French roux.

You need a command of English to express yourself during future TED talks, explain your Ferrari's engine problems to the mechanic, write C.E.O reports, and concisely convey your brilliant ideas in university papers.

English is the language of international communication, so the more proficient you are, the more you will excel in the global market.

If your career ambitions do not include slinging fries in a fast food joint, you need English. Relax! I'm here to make the process of improving writing skills easy and enjoyable. Have a delicious Word burger with Caesar salad and a side of fries on me.

Content Issues

The ailment: Fuzzy thinking caused by sleep deprivation.

If a teacher can ask questions about your sentence, you have not explained the points clearly and will see the comments *vague* or *unclear* on your essay. The worst trap to fall into is using *"Wh" clauses*. I have named them death trap constructions because they look correct but are meaningless.

Examples of death traps are *what they did, whom she saw* and *why he did it*. Using vague pronouns such as *they* does not help.

 The remedy: A good night's sleep.

To escape the trap, ask questions. Who are they? What happened? Where did they live? Replace these constructions with concrete nouns and verbs.

Weak: They were upset because of what happened on the island.

Clear: The young children on the deserted island in Lord of the Flies are terrified, for the older leaders become savages and slaughter the younger ones.

Weak: He didn't like where he lived.

Clear: Tom loathed living in Toronto, for the filthy flurries infuriated him.

Weak: She wondered what the man was doing.

Clear: Tina wondered why Fritz was jogging in shorts during a blizzard.

Words are Bones

Imagine walking without bones in your body.

What would you look like? Jell-o? Would you wobble your way to school like a worm? How would your skeleton support your body without a solid bone structure?

Words are the bones and structure of a good sentence. Without strong words, your sentences will fail to support your ideas.

The ailment: The exhausted and overused word *people*.

The word *people* is boring and vague. To make sentences scintillating, ask yourself *which people*.

Weak: These days, many *people* are worried about what they are going to do later in life.

 The remedy: Be specific.

Today, *students* are concerned about employment prospects.

Tourists adoringly admired the
statues in the Louvre.

Scientists are quietly cloning genes in secret labs.

Practice: How many new words can you brainstorm to
replace the word *people*?

Challenge yourself! You have three minutes to write your
dazzling brainstorm. You will receive 3 points for every
word. Be original and have fun!

Here are some sample ideas: Doctors, protestors,
inventors, laggards, civilians, soldiers, warriors, anar-
chists, witches, warlocks, toddlers, tattlers, coaches, ath-
letes, superstars, peanut, lunatics, researchers, labour-
ers, landlords, adolescents, undertakers, waitresses,
citizens. You get the drift.

How did you score?

100 points or more: You are a creative genius.

50-75 points: Don't be embarrassed. You secretly love
this activity.

50 points or less: By the time you complete the exercises
in this book, you will score over a hundred points.

Did you find the word *peanut*? Genius! Score another
50 points!

Redundant and
Illogical Definitions

The ailment: Redundancy.

Repeating yourself ad nauseum will give you heartburn. Do not use the phrases *is when, is where, reason why* or the worst culprit, *the reason why is because*.

The remedy: Begin sentences with clear subjects.

Weak: In the novel *Of Mice and Men*, the reason why Lennie has poor judgment is because he is mentally challenged.

Clear: In the novel *Of Mice and Men, Lennie* (subject) has poor judgment because he is mentally challenged.

The ailment: Ill- defined terms

Do not use *is when* or *is where* to define a term.

The remedy: A shot of logical thinking

When depicts time and *where* suggests location. A place cannot be a time.

Weak: University *is when* you finish high school.

Clear: A university *is an institution for advanced education*.

Weak: A revolution *is when* a bunch of angry people riot.

Clear: A revolution *is a state of political anarchy* caused by dissidents overthrowing an oppressive system.

Practice: Rewrite these illogical sentences.

Culture is when different people come together and the reason conflict occurs is because of this.

There are three reasons why school is an important place to be.

Science is when a bunch of people do experiments in a lab.

Do as I Say and You Shall Receive an A!

Dict, Dicere: Latin root *to say*:

A dictator: One who says too much.

Dictionary: A great bathroom read.

Diction: Word choice.

The ailment: A bad case of the blah's.

In essays, do not write using conversational words. If your word choice is too casual, you will see the following terms on your paper.

Colloquial: Natural spoken English.

The soldier *kicked the bucket* during the war.

Slang: Language considered ungrammatical in speaking and writing.

Me and him went to the mall.

 The remedy: Change diction from blah to bling.

Replace casual words with appropriate diction.

Kid: Baby, child, adolescent, teenager, juvenile.

Mom, Dad: Mother, father.

The main dude, the guy, the girl: The protagonist, the antagonist, the speaker, the character.

Cool, interesting: Enchanting, brilliant, talented, fascinating.

Pissed: Frustrated, dismayed, perturbed, annoyed.

Offed: Murdered, killed, assassinated, stabbed.

Show, Don't Tell

Do you remember Show and Tell day when you were a child? I recall bringing squirming minnows to class much to my teacher's surprise.

The ailment: A headache.

When teachers ask you to write a descriptive paragraph, you can't understand the concept and feel a migraine coming on.

Read the two passages below. Get some paper and draw the images that come to mind. Yes, *draw* the place described in each passage.

Which passage can you picture easily and why?

Victoria is a really nice place to visit, and lots of tourists like it because it has good weather. There are many activities to do and it has great scenery. Downtown is also nice and it's easy to get around. Because of all the things to do, I recommend visiting Victoria on Vancouver Island as it is pretty.

Imagine being in a horse drawn carriage clopping through the historic centre of Victoria. The cobblestone streets echo the sound of horse hooves. Colourful flower baskets dangle from cast iron lampposts. The granny, the Empress hotel, is an impressive ivy covered landmark facing the inner harbour. She wearily watches shuttle boats scoot like insects across the water, ferrying passengers. At night, the Parliament building resembles a fairy castle, shimmering with tiny white lights. Victoria, the garden city, is a must see on lush and verdant Vancouver Island. I recommend visiting Victoria.

Which paragraph was easy to draw and which one was impossible to illustrate?

Why was the second paragraph easy to visualize?

Which words evoked pictures, feelings and sounds in your mind?

The remedy: Don't skip breakfast.

To avoid sugar crash headaches, do not use junk food filler in your writing. Steer clear of *good, bad, nice, interesting, pretty, thing, different,* and other empty calories. Abstract words are hard to picture and make your writing dreary. Ask yourself *in what way* Victoria is nice, pretty, interesting or bad.. Pretend you are in a movie when you describe a place. Include colours, textures, sounds, and pictures such as *cobblestone streets* (visual) and *horse hooves clopping* (sound) to make your writing spring to life. Readers should be able to see the pictures and feel as if they are in your story. Roll the camera!

Movement and Momentum

You are playing rugby and receive a pass. Sprinting with the ball, you feel a sharp pain in your foot, and stop three feet from the goal. Instead of hobbling across the line and scoring a goal, you are mercilessly tackled by the opponents.

The ailment: A sprained ankle.

Once you have set the ball in motion, keep running. Your essay loses momentum when your *ideas* spiral downward from specific details to general statements.

Example of strong to weak sentences:

Shakespeare's play Romeo and Juliet contains implicit warnings about impulsive behaviour. The besotted teens recklessly elope, with no sense of the consequences. Teenagers don't know anything because they are too young. They get into trouble and do stupid things.

Which sentences are strong?

Draw a red line at the point at which this paragraph loses steam.

The remedy: An ice pack.

After the topic sentence, prove points and do not make general statements after specific ones. If teachers can ask *why*, *how*, or *in what way*, you have not proven your points clearly.

A healthy formula for writing includes one strong point per paragraph with three to four *supporting details* which are more specific than the main idea or topic sentence. Students lose the most marks by omitting detailed analysis. *Do not lose momentum* by moving from specific ideas to general ones.

Anxiety Attack

The ailment: Nail biting and nervous writing.

Other teensy weensy problems with momentum and pacing are caused by repeating a lot of filling, little itsy bitsy repetitive words. Anxious writers compensate for lack of content by stuffing in a few extra words like itsy-bitsy to fill their essays.

 The remedy: Stop using word count.

One powerful word is worth more than a hundred wimpy ones. *Remove all unnecessary words.*

Weak: These days, it seems to me like each and every single student doesn't know what to do when he or she gets out of school.

Clear: Students are worried about employment opportunities after graduation.

Weak: All over the world, it is really important that every single person on the planet goes to school to get an education.

Clear: Today, all over the world, education is crucial.

Practice: Ruthlessly remove words until these sentences are manicured.

In this day and age, a lot of people today think about all the different kinds of pollution that we are doing to the planet.

Another reason that there are so many problems in the world today is that people are fighting against each other over things like religion.

Clutter Busting

The ailment: Tripping over verbs.

Walking through your bedroom, you find yourself tripping over hockey sticks, piles of books, several pairs of boots, dirty laundry and a bag of garbage. How annoying!

When your sentences have multiple, meaningless verbs, readers trip over the first verb and can't find the clear message you wish to convey.

 The remedy: Clean your room.

Use one strong verb and do not write *start to, begin to,* or *try to* in essays because less is more. Go straight for the meaty verb.

Trippy: Atticus Finch *started to try to help* Tom Robinson, but it didn't go very well.

Clear: Atticus Finch *defends* Tom Robinson in court, for Tom is innocent, but the racist civilians *threaten to lynch* the black man.

Trippy: Macbeth was mad and *started to think* all the time about how to murder Duncan.

Clear: Macbeth malevolently *contemplated murdering* his nemesis, Duncan.

Practice: Clean up the clutter in these sentences.

Romeo and Juliet start to make a plan to elope, but when they try to run away together, they begin to have problems.

Today it seems like a lot of people are starting to go back to school to try to improve their chances of getting a better job.

Wash Your Hands:
The Virus is Spreading!

The ailment: The word *different*.

The adjective *different* is a contagious word which needs to be contained. After using the word *different* in your topic sentence, don't repeat it.

The essay topic is *Compare an event in two cultures*. Here is the student's first body paragraph.

Different cultures have different ways of doing things because they all think differently. Some cultures have other traditions and they are different from ours. That's why we all like different things.

The prognosis for the teacher marking this paragraph is brain death.

To rid yourself of the plague, ask yourself *in what way* culture A is different from culture B?

The remedy: Revive your sentences with concrete examples.

For some Christians, Christmas in North America is the most important celebration of the year. Families congregate to attend church, exchange presents and enjoy traditional turkey dinner. On the other hand, Chinese New Year is the most symbolic event in Asia. Families share elaborate meals of fresh seafood to symbolize new beginnings. Other rituals include lighting fireworks and giving children red envelopes containing money to promote prosperity and good luck.

Wimpy Language

The ailment: Weak and wimpy verbs

Avoid two part verbs and use one strong verb. Two part verbs are not ungrammatical, but weak and wordy.

The cure: Replace flabby phrases with a six pack verb.

Look up to him a lot	Respect, admire, idolize
Go out of the house	Leave, depart
Went up to and said hi	Introduced herself
Can't stand	Dislike, loathe, despise
Put up with	Tolerate
Think about	Ponder, consider, evaluate
Get rid of	Destroy, eliminate, eradicate
Get it	Understand, comprehend
Go against	Disobey, rebel, protest
Look at	Observe, examine, scrutinize
Go after	Pursue, chase

Do You Have This-itis?

The ailment: Bland writing from using empty subjects.

The remedy: Use spicy nouns for flavour.

English is a subject-verb-object language and adheres strictly to this word order. Thus, sentences must begin with proper nouns. In Mandarin, one can say "Raining", but English requires a word to save the subject position. Empty subjects such as *it* and *this,* however, have no meaning and make sentences weak. Use dynamic words to replace these empty subjects which merely hold the subject position.

Weak: *It* is quite cold out today.

Clear: *The cold, miserable rain* made her bones ache.

Weak: *It* is bad when people can't pay their bills because things are expensive.

Clear: *Inflation* squeezes the poor, who can't afford food.

Weak: *This* won't hurt a bit.

Clear: *Writing clearly* won't hurt a bit.

Weak: This creates problems for Mrs Mallard.

Clear: *Her unhappy marriage* creates problems for Mrs Mallard.

Skeletons in the Closet:
The Essay Outline

Now that you are the master of words and can write sentences with solid bone structure, it's time to construct the skeleton: The outline.

Why do I need an outline?

Outlines organize your thoughts and provide structure. You can't build a house without an architectural blueprint, and you will waste time and energy if you do not clearly outline your points.

What should I include in my outline?

Your outline should include the thesis, and 3-5 points to develop.

How do I write the introductory paragraph?

Write a one sentence hook, a summary of the story, poem, or material, followed by the title and author's name, and the thesis. Keep it short! Three clear sentences is enough.

Topic: Discuss the speaker's changing attitudes in the poem.

Example: Childhood is a time of wonder as Peter Smith's poem *My Awakening* depicts. In this piece, a young boy's pet dies, causing him to mature and lose interest in childish games. The poem uses imagery and figurative language to convey the changing attitudes of the speaker.

For a one page essay prompt, you need an introductory paragraph with a hook, background information and topic sentence, and three to five examples supported by quotations and proof in the main body of each paragraph. Every essay needs a brief conclusion.

What is the difference between a thesis and a topic sentence?

A **thesis** contains the argument or ideas developed in an essay.

A **topic sentence** is derived from the thesis and develops the main idea of a paragraph.

Thesis: For urban dwellers, having a pet cat is preferable to a dog because cats are tidy, discreet and independent.

The thesis has two parts: The *controlling idea* is that a cat is a better city pet than a dog.

The *plan of development* lists three points which will be developed in three body paragraphs.

The *topic sentences* will begin with these three points:

1) Cats are tidy.

2) Cats are discreet.

3) Cats are independent.

As you write your paragraphs, avoid repeating the same words used in the topic sentences by using synonyms. It's a good idea to brainstorm a list of related words prior to writing the paragraphs.

Try thinking of a few synonyms for the three words used here - tidy, discreet, independent.

Plot Summary and Analytical Writing

What is the difference between plot summary and analytical writing?

Plot summary merely states the action and conclusion of a story or play, without proving the thesis or analysing the information.

The ailment: Stating the obvious. If your essay is largely plot summary, or you insert quotations without explaining their relevance, you will not receive marks.

Plot summary:

Story of an Hour by Kate Chopin is about a woman who secretly does not love her husband. She finds out that her husband has died in a train accident, and cries in her room. Suddenly, she stops crying and realizes she is free. Her brother in law and sister don't know that Mrs Mallard is happy that Brentley is dead. At the end of the story, Brentley arrives home and doesn't know anything had happened. Mrs Mallard drops dead.

 The remedy: An injection of analysis.

In *Story of An Hour* by Kate Chopin, Mrs. Mallard, the protagonist, discovers that her husband has died in a train accident. Her relatives shield her from excessive stress due to her heart condition, and she retreats to her room. Initially, Mrs Mallard cries "with wild abandon" but as she observes the sky clearing, her emotions also calm. She questions her relationship with her husband, and admits that "often she had not loved him." She discovers that nothing matters more than her "self-assertion" or independence which she has never experienced in her oppressive marriage. Mrs Mallard whispers furtively, "free, free body and soul free", a phrase scandalous for its time in the late 1800's. Her liberty is short lived. When her husband returns home oblivious to news of the accident, Mrs Mallard dies of "joy that kills", taking her secret grief to the grave.

Narrowing A.C.T and S.A.T. Essay Topics

The ailment: Your mind cannot grasp the slippery prompt.

The S.A.T and A.C.T tests have a general prompt in the assignment which you are expected to *narrow to a thesis statement*. It is crucial to reword the prompt and create a clear thesis.

Sample S.A.T assignment: *People find it hard to change what they believe.*

Did this prompt make your brain spin in circles?

The phrase *what they believe* is a death trap construction; so your mind has no concrete noun to anchor it, and you will struggle to find ideas.

 The remedy: Apply the questioning technique you learned to fix fuzzy thinking.

What exactly do people find hard to change? Change the question into a statement and answer the prompt.

People find it hard to change their *attitudes, ideas, values and beliefs*.

Now, rewrite the prompt and turn it into a question: *What is an example of an idea or belief* that people find hard to change, and which *people*?

Atheists find it hard to believe *that God exists*, for atheists hold a scientific point of view based on evolution.

Conservative Catholics find it hard to change *their religious beliefs*, for their convictions are ingrained from childhood.

Citizens *who have not been abducted by aliens* find *alien conspiracies* hard to believe.

Abused children may find it hard to believe that they are worthy if they have been neglected.

Afterword

I hope that you have enjoyed using my exercises as much as I enjoyed creating them. My writing tips have been culled from over twenty years of experience teaching, correcting content errors, making suggestions, and observing my students' grades rapidly improve. You can breathe a sigh of relief that those itchy red marks have disappeared from your papers. Congratulations!

I'd love to hear your comments or questions. For more information and grammar tips, visit my website at www.lindsayclewis.com. I can be contacted at info@ lindsayclewis.com for my extensive English services including public speaking, grammar workshops, book editing, international workshops, grammar slams and private lessons.

Dedications

I am deeply grateful to my late parents: My mother Beryl encouraged my love of reading and literature at an early age, and my father Iystyn was my best friend and mentor, always cheering me on with his tremendous support and ebullient optimism.

Many thanks to my brother Nick for igniting my incendiary imagination by feeding me ee.cummings poetry and Shakespeare when I was a fledgling writer, and for his invaluable editorial expertise.

To my lifer friends: Morgan and Jeff Savin, Janice Kelliher, Victoria Clarke, Tracy Kelher, Michelle Schevkenek , Kathy Roth, Peter Gardiner, Becky Reed, Karoline Guelke and Planet Janet, Dania Frame, and Linda Neville, thank you for your love, hugs, support, wine nights, inspiration, walks and friendship.

I also wish to thank Kim Oldham and Dogbless Rescue for their tireless work and for saving my little daemon, Ella.

To my inspiring kids, current and former students: You are my extended family. Thank you for sharing your personal and academic journeys with me.

About the Author

Lindsay Lewis holds a degree in Applied Linguistics and a Cambridge teaching diploma from England. She has been teaching English and English as a Second Language at colleges, universities and private schools since 1994. She specializes in grammar, essay writing, literature, poetry, SAT, and exam preparation. Passionate about language, Ms. Lewis models correct writing with students so they can correct errors and see their writing and grades rapidly improve. Residing in Victoria, B.C., Ms. Lewis is currently recording a grammar blues song and working on a travel memoir entitled *"Biscotti Bites"*.

Photo by Victoria Clarke

CPSIA information can be obtained at www.ICGtesting.com
Printed in the USA
LVOW06*2300111215

465720LV00002B/14/P

9 781460 272206